Man Ray

A BOOK OF POSTCARDS

Pomegranate

SAN FRANCISCO

Pomegranate Communications, Inc.
Box 808022, Petaluma CA 94975
800 227 1428; www.pomegranate.com

Pomegranate Europe Ltd.
Unit 1, Heathcote Business Centre, Hurlbutt Road
Warwick, Warwickshire CV34 6TD, UK
[+44] 0 1926 430111; sales@pomeurope.co.uk

ISBN 978-0-7649-5055-1
Pomegranate Catalog No. AA597

Pomegranate publishes books of postcards on a wide range of subjects.
Please contact the publisher for more information.

Cover designed by Shannon Lemme
Printed in Korea
21 20 19 18 17 16 15 14 13 12   11 10 9 8 7 6 5 4 3 2

To facilitate detachment of the postcards from this book, fold each card along its perforation line before tearing.

Man Ray was born Emmanuel Radnitsky in Philadelphia, Pennsylvania, on August 27, 1890, the son of Russian-Jewish immigrants. The family moved to Brooklyn, New York, in 1897. An avid artist from an early age, Man Ray worked as a commercial artist and illustrator after graduating from high school. Studies at the Art Students League, the National Academy of Design, and the progressive Ferrer Center gave him a taste for the avant-garde, which was further fueled by a visit to the Armory Show in 1913. By 1915 Man Ray had earned his first solo exhibition of paintings and drawings. A friendship with French artist Marcel Duchamp sparked an interest in the nascent Dada movement, which led him to experiments with assemblages and found objects. Then around 1918, inspired by the photography and other modern work he had seen at Alfred Steiglitz's New York gallery, he turned to the camera as a primary art-making tool.

In 1921, Man Ray moved to Paris, where his career flourished. He met and photographed such contemporary icons as Gertrude Stein, James Joyce, Ernest Hemingway, and Antonin Artaud, and his flair for portraiture led to commercial fashion photography assignments for *Vogue* and *Harper's Bazaar.* In 1925 his personal work was included in the first Surrealist exhibition alongside that of Pablo Picasso, Joan Miró, Max Ernst, and others. Also in the 1920s, Man Ray directed a number of his own avant-garde short films and assisted in others by fellow artists Duchamp and Fernand Léger.

Always exploring new avenues of artistic expression, Man Ray became well known for his photograms (which he called "Rayographs," made by placing objects directly atop unexposed photographic printing paper, then exposing the paper to light) and his trademark solarizations (made by exposing partially developed photographic prints or negatives to a brief flash of light, resulting in reversed tones and fine lines between areas of high contrast).

World War II forced Man Ray to leave Paris. He moved to Hollywood, California, and continued painting, object-making, and working as a fashion photographer until 1951, when he returned to his beloved Montparnasse. He remained there until his death in 1976. Today Man Ray is appreciated as an innovative artist of enormous imagination and curiosity, who eschewed formal constraints and set his creative spirit free to play at will.

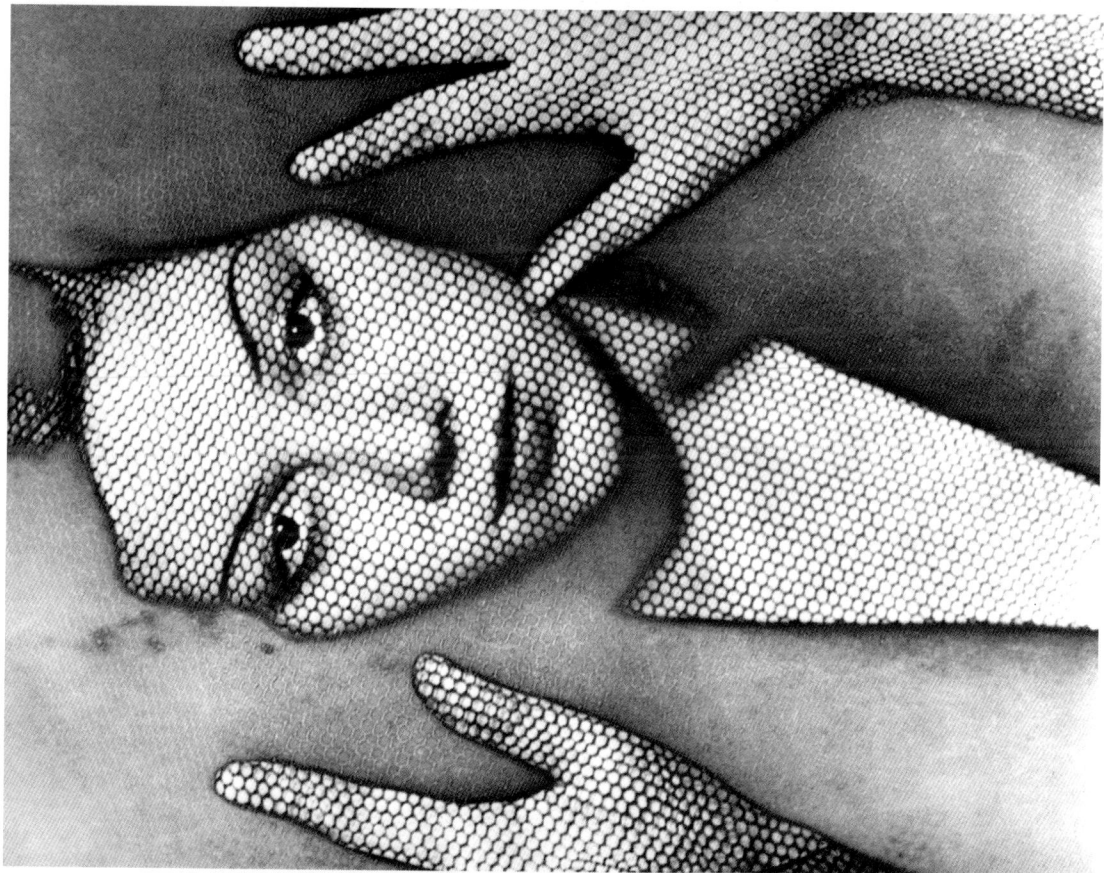

Man Ray (American, 1890–1976)
La Résille, 1931
Solarized gelatin silver print

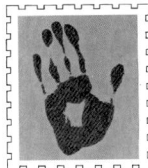

707 782 9000   WWW.POMEGRANATE.COM

Pomegranate

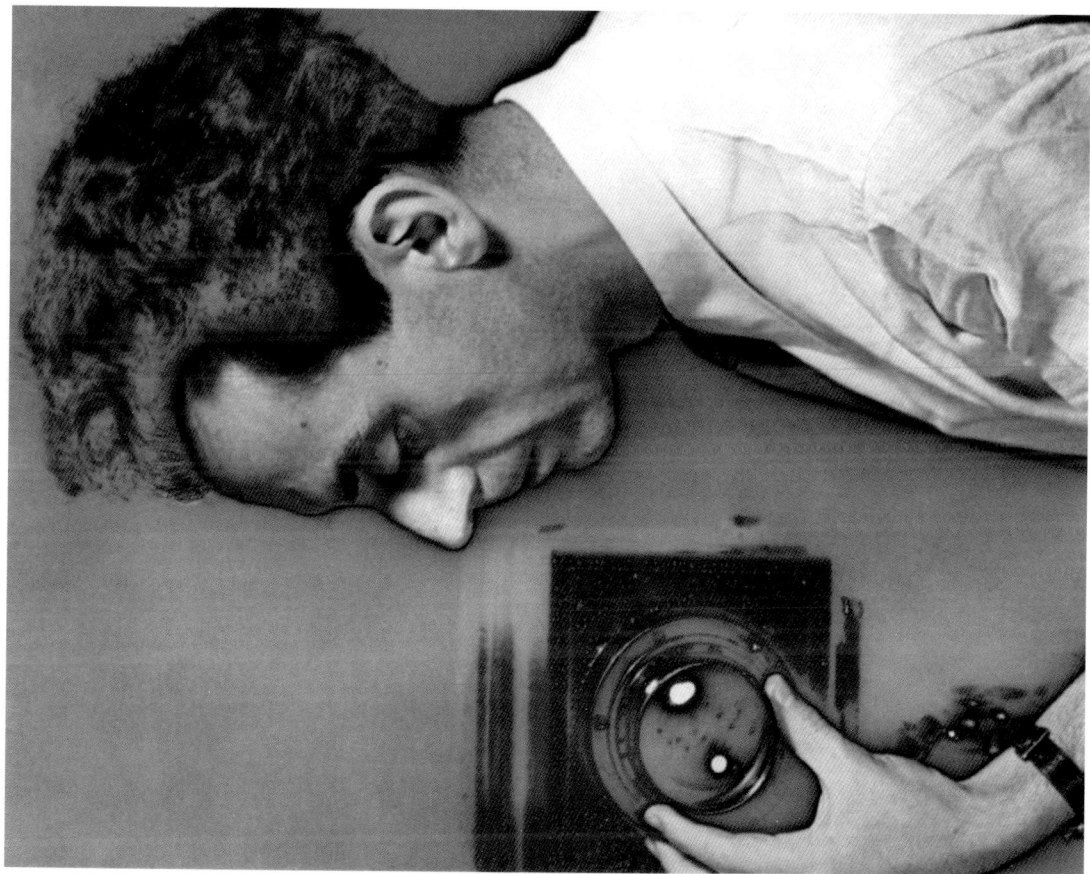

Man Ray (American, 1890–1976)
Untitled (Self-portrait with camera), 1930, printed c. 1935
Solarized gelatin silver print, 4¾ x 3½ in. (12.1 x 8.9 cm)
The Jewish Museum, New York
Purchase: Photography Acquisitions Committee Fund,
Horace W. Goldsmith Fund, and Jack Stern Gift, 2004-16
The Jewish Museum is under the auspices of The Jewish
Theological Seminary of America

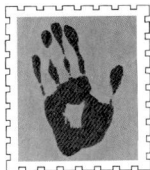

707 782 9000 WWW.POMEGRANATE.COM

Pomegranate

Man Ray (American, 1890–1976)
Promenade, 1915
Gouache

707 782 9000   WWW.POMEGRANATE.COM

Pomegranate

Man Ray (American, 1890–1976)
War (AD MCMXIV), 1914
Oil on canvas
Philadelphia Museum of Art

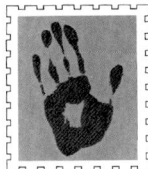

707 782 9000   WWW.POMEGRANATE.COM

Pomegranate

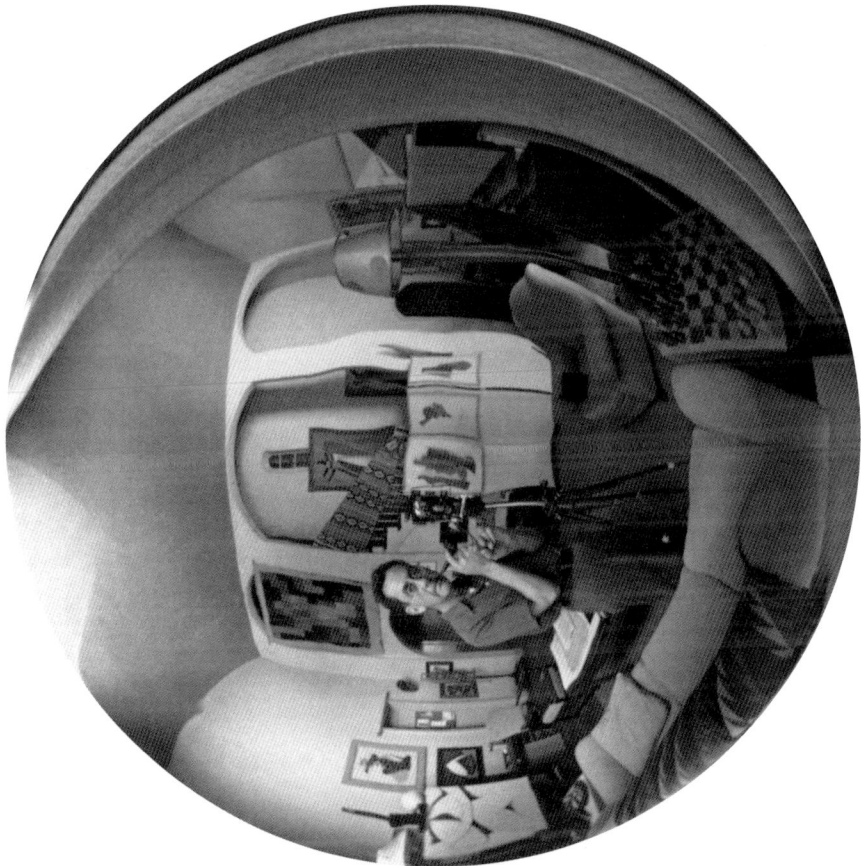

Man Ray (American, 1890–1976)
Self-portrait, Hollywood, 1944
Gelatin silver print

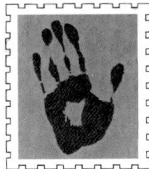

707 782 9000   WWW.POMEGRANATE.COM

Pomegranate

Man Ray (American, 1890–1976)
Kiki de Montparnasse, 1926
Gelatin silver print

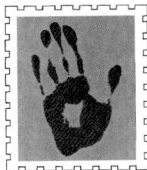

707 782 9000   WWW.POMEGRANATE.COM

Pomegranate

Man Ray (American, 1890–1976)
Le Beau Temps, 1939
Oil on canvas

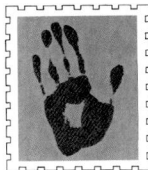

WWW.POMEGRANATE.COM

707 782 9000

Pomegranate

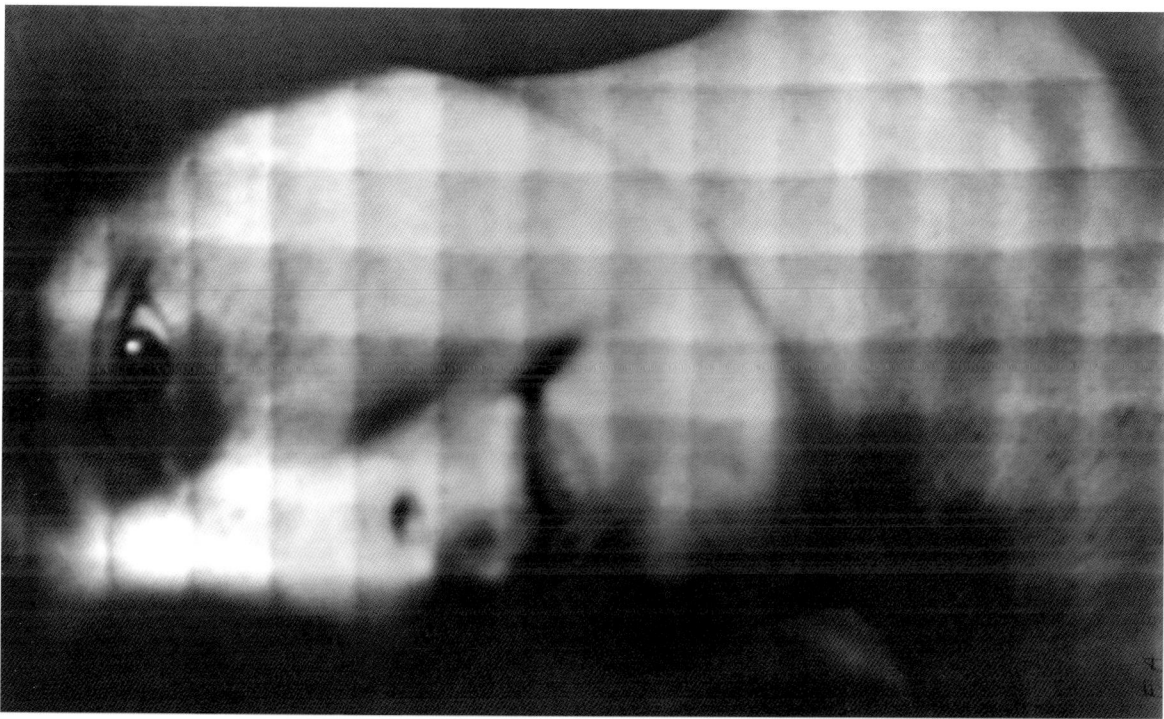

Man Ray (American, 1890–1976)
Dada Portrait, 1920–1921
Gelatin silver print

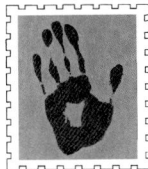

707 782 9000   WWW.POMEGRANATE.COM

Pomegranate

Man Ray (American, 1890–1976)
Nuit de Saint-Jean-de-Luz, 1968
Lithograph

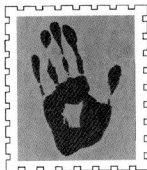

707 782 9000 WWW.POMEGRANATE.COM

Pomegranate

MAN RAY '26

Man Ray (American, 1890–1976)
Noire et blanche (Kiki de Montparnasse), 1926
Gelatin silver print

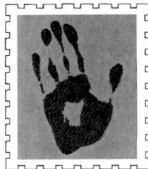

707 782 9000   WWW.POMEGRANATE.COM

Pomegranate

Man Ray (American, 1890–1976)
Optical Longings and Illusions
Lithograph, after 1943 gouache, ink wash, and collage
on paperboard

707 782 9000   WWW.POMEGRANATE.COM

Pomegranate

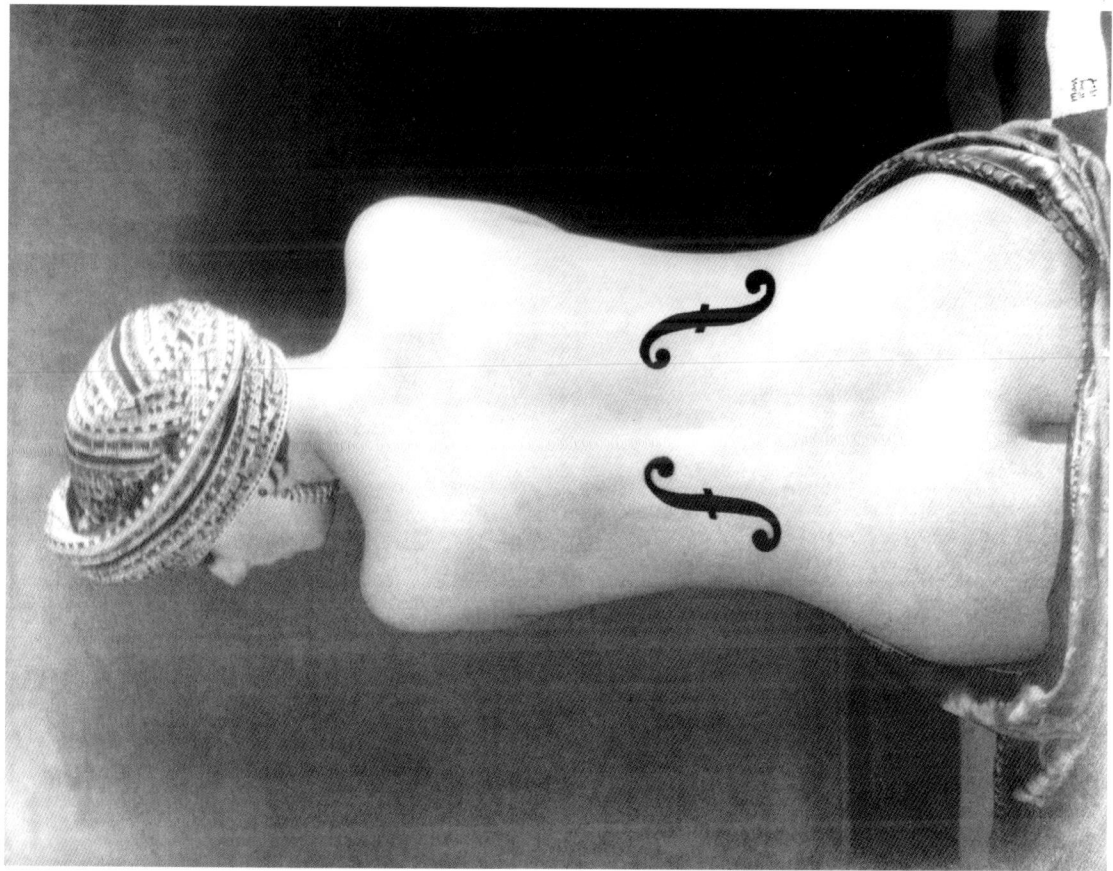

Man Ray (American, 1890–1976)
Le Violon d'Ingres, 1924
Gelatin silver print

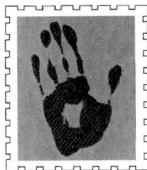

707 782 9000   WWW.POMEGRANATE.COM

Pomegranate

Man Ray (American, 1890–1976)
Jean Cocteau with Self-portrait Wire Sculpture, 1926
Gelatin silver print

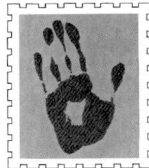

Pomegranate

707 782 9000   WWW.POMEGRANATE.COM

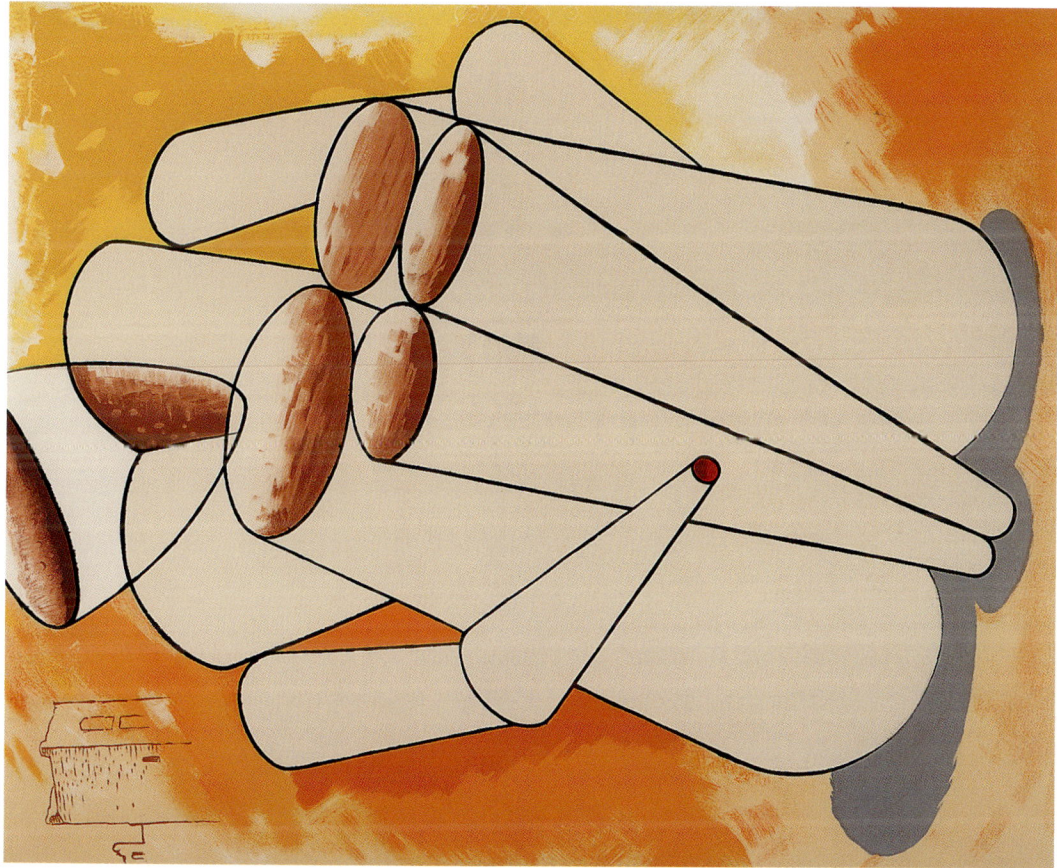

Man Ray (American, 1890–1976)
Untitled, 1939
Lithograph

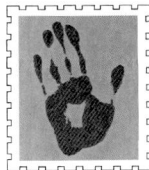

707 782 9000   WWW.POMEGRANATE.COM

Pomegranate

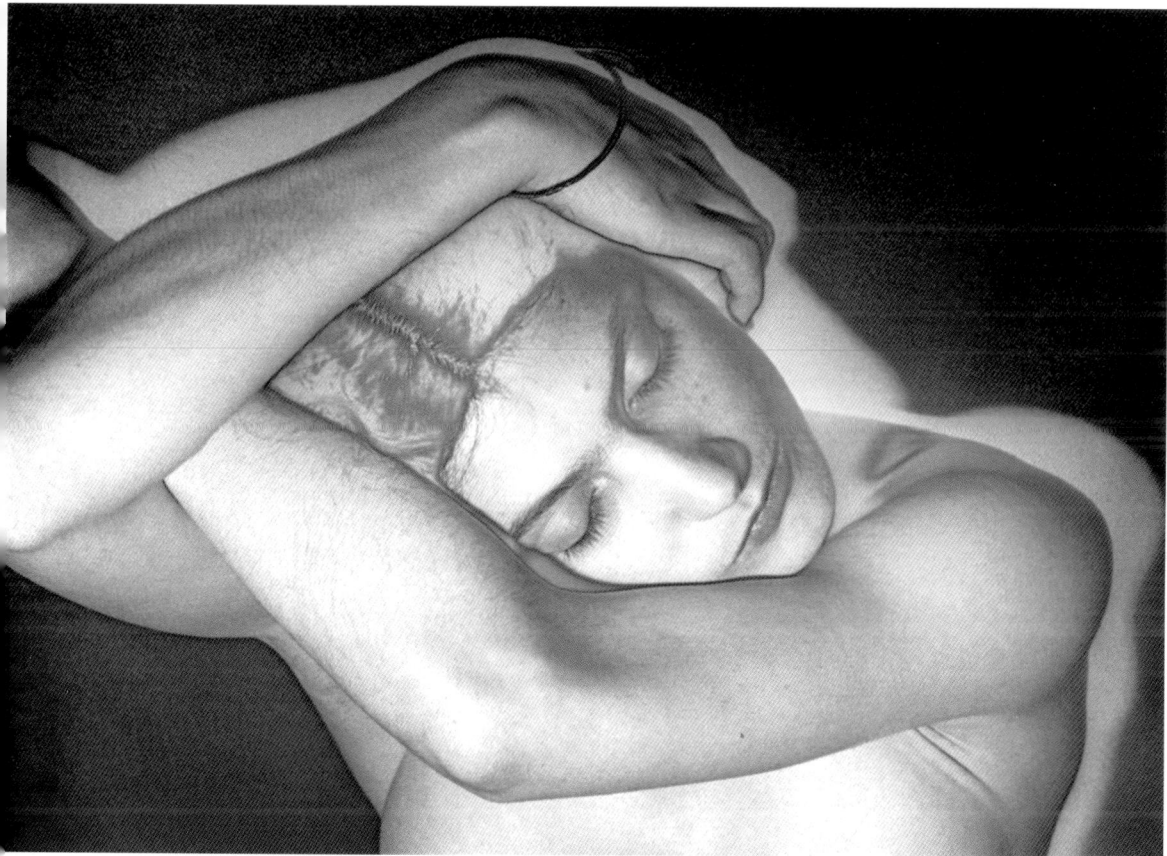

Man Ray (American, 1890–1976)
Untitled, 1931
Solarized gelatin silver print

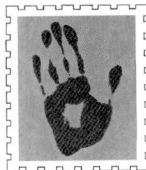

707 782 9000   WWW.POMEGRANATE.COM

Pomegranate

Man Ray (American, 1890–1976)
Alice B. Toklas and Gertrude Stein (27 rue Fleurus, Paris), 1922
Gelatin silver print

707 782 9000   WWW.POMEGRANATE.COM

Pomegranate

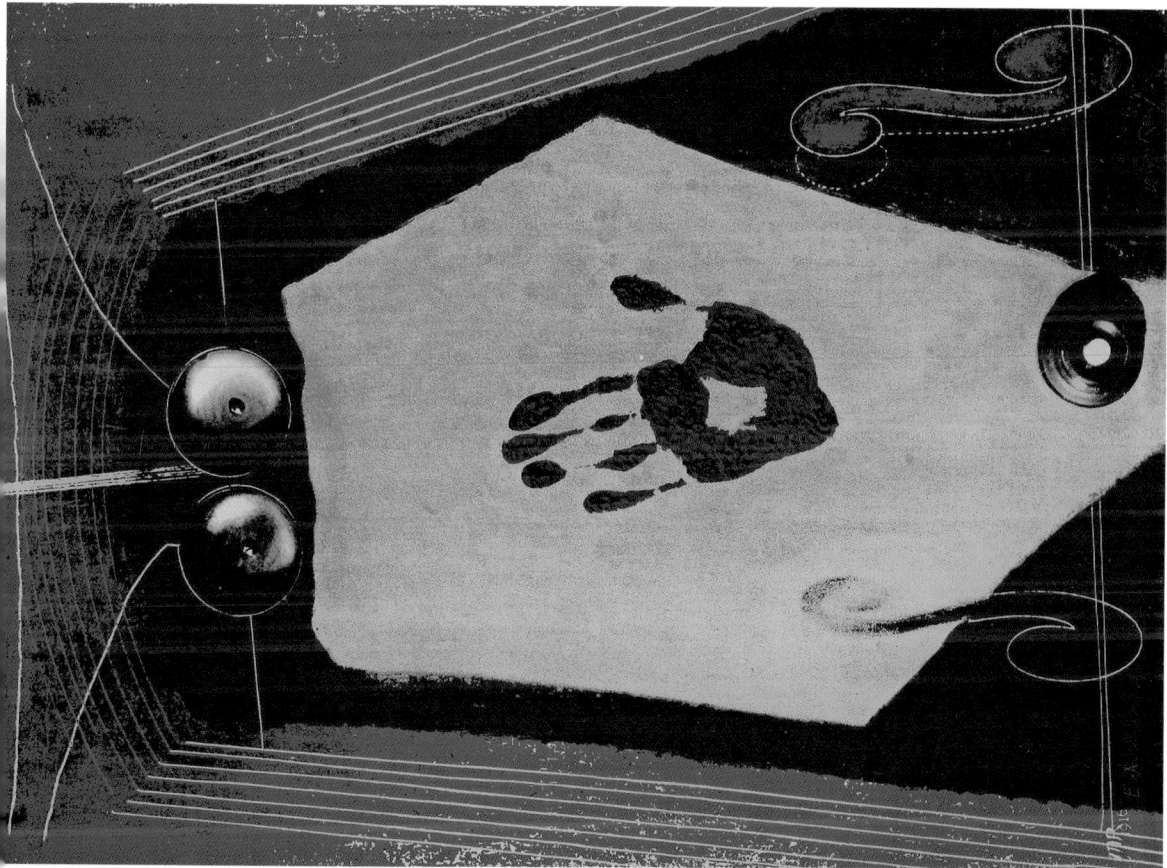

Man Ray (American, 1890–1976)
Autoportrait, 1916
Photomechanical reproduction on plastic, laminated to
acrylic glass

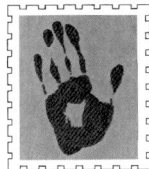

707 782 9000 WWW.POMEGRANATE.COM

Pomegranate

DANGER

L'IMPOSSIBLE

MAN RAY
1920

Man Ray (American, 1890–1976)
L'Impossible, 1920
Serigraph on plastic

707 782 9000   WWW.POMEGRANATE.COM

Pomegranate

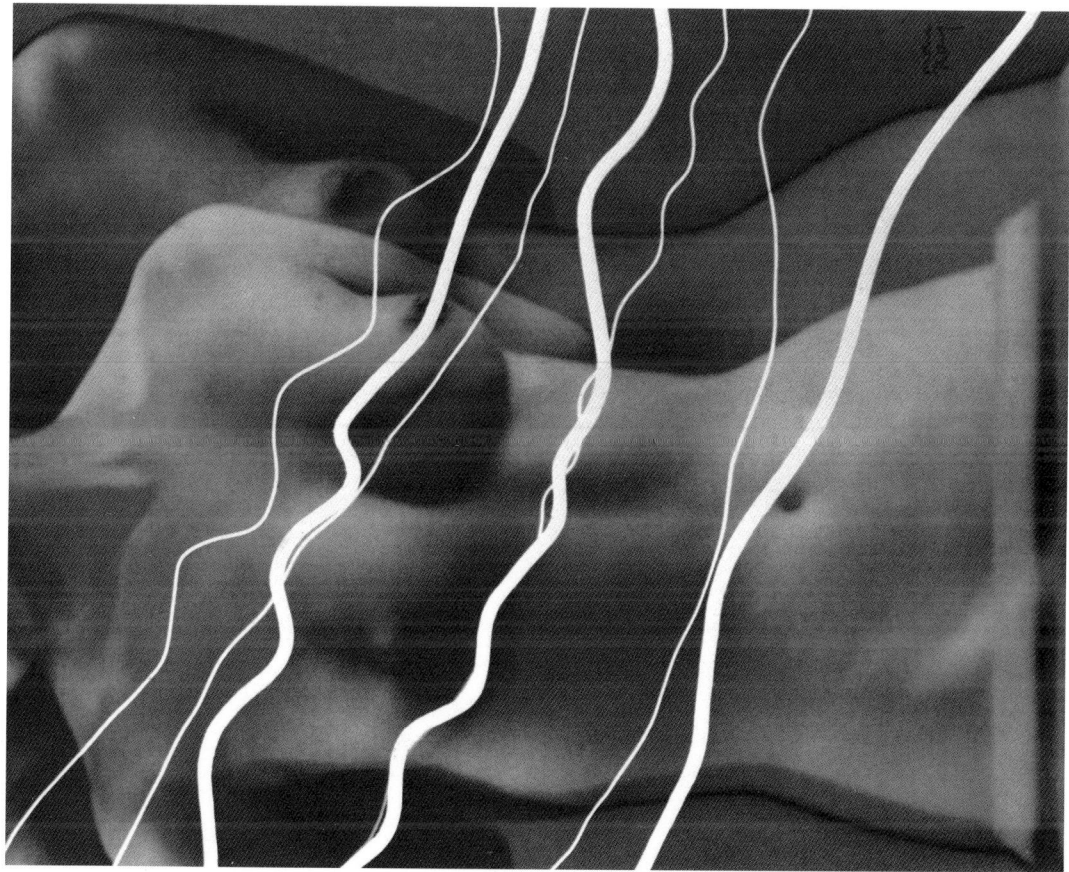

Man Ray (American, 1890–1976)
Torso, 1931
Rayograph (photogram) gelatin silver print, from the
portfolio "Electricité"

707 782 9000 WWW.POMEGRANATE.COM

Pomegranate

MAN RAY
1952

Man Ray (American, 1890–1976)
La Rue Férou
Lithograph, after 1952 oil on canvas

707 782 9000   WWW.POMEGRANATE.COM

Pomegranate

Man Ray (American, 1890–1976)
Dora Marr, 1936
Solarized gelatin silver print

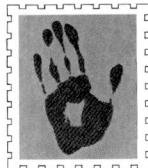

707 782 9000   WWW.POMEGRANATE.COM

Pomegranate

Man Ray (American, 1890–1976)
Image à deux faces
Lithograph, after 1959 oil on canvas

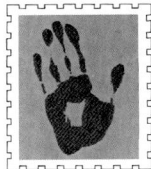

707 782 9000 WWW.POMEGRANATE.COM

Pomegranate

Man Ray (American, 1890–1976)
Jacqueline Goddard, 1932
Gelatin silver print

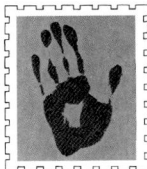

707 782 9000   WWW.POMEGRANATE.COM

Pomegranate

Man Ray (American, 1890–1976)
Untitled, 1935
Solarized gelatin silver print

707 782 9000   WWW.POMEGRANATE.COM

Pomegranate

man Ray

Man Ray (American, 1890–1976)
Seguidilla
Lithograph, after 1919 airbrushed gouache with pen and ink,
pencil, and colored pencil on paperboard

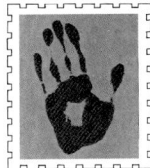

707 782 9000   WWW.POMEGRANATE.COM

Pomegranate

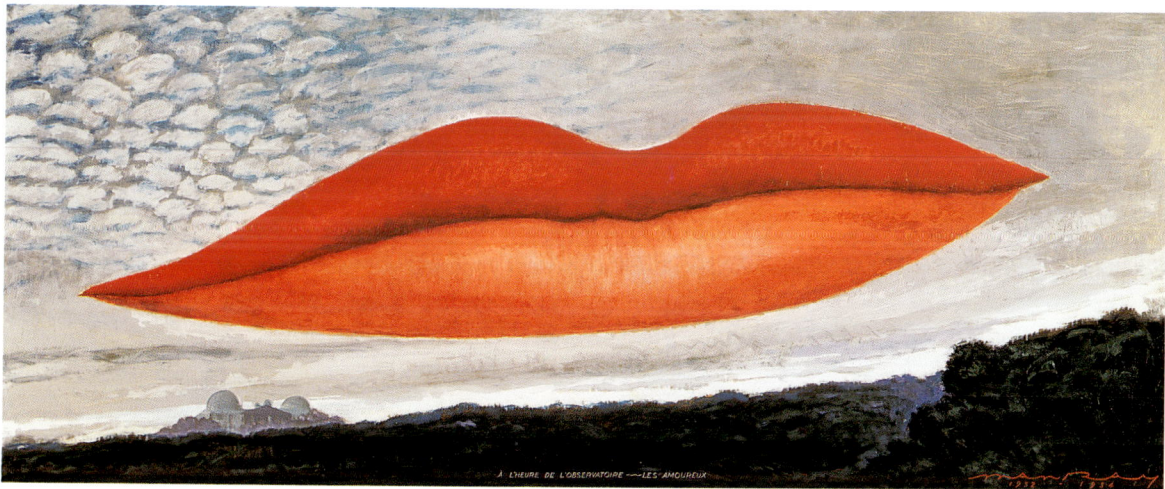

À L'HEURE DE L'OBSERVATOIRE ---LES AMOUREUX

Man Ray (American, 1890–1976)
À l'heure de l'observatoire—Les Amoureux, 1932–1934
Oil on canvas
Niarchos Collection

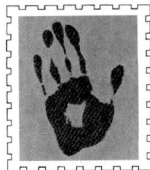

707 782 9000   WWW.POMEGRANATE.COM

Pomegranate

Man Ray (American, 1890–1976)
La Fortune
Lithograph, after 1938 oil on canvas

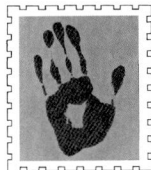

707 782 9000   WWW.POMEGRANATE.COM

Pomegranate